STEM *trailblazer* BIOS

NUCLEAR PHYSICIST
CHIEN-SHIUNG WU

VALERIE BODDEN

Lerner Publications ◆ Minneapolis

Lerner Publications Company
A division of Lerner Publishing Group, Inc.
241 First Avenue North
Minneapolis, MN 55401 U.S.A.

For reading levels and more information, look up this title at www.lernerbooks.com.

Content Consultant: Aimee Slaughter, Museum Educator, Los Alamos Historical Society

Library of Congress Cataloging-in-Publication Data

Names: Bodden, Valerie, author.
Title: Nuclear physicist Chien-Shiung Wu / by Valerie Bodden.
Other titles: STEM trailblazer bios.
Description: Minneapolis : Lerner Publications, [2017] | Series: STEM trailblazer bios | Includes
    bibliographical references and index.
Identifiers: LCCN 2016002988 (print) | LCCN 2016008355 (ebook) | ISBN 9781512407860 (lb : alk.
    paper) | ISBN 9781512413069 (pb : alk. paper) | ISBN 9781512410891 (eb pdf)
Subjects: LCSH: Wu, C. S. (Chien-shiung), 1912–1997—Juvenile literature. | Manhattan Project
    (U.S.)—Juvenile literature. | Chinese American women—Biography—Juvenile literature. | Chinese
    Americans—Biography—Juvenile literature. | Women physicists—Biography—Juvenile literature. |
    Physicists—Biography—Juvenile literature. | Physics—History—20th century—Juvenile literature.
Classification: LCC QC16.W785 B63 2017 (print) | LCC QC16.W785 (ebook) | DDC 530.092—dc23

LC record available at http://lccn.loc.gov/2016002988

Manufactured in the United States of America
1 – PC – 7/15/16

The images in this book are used with the permission of: © SPL/Science Source, p. 4; © qingqing/
Shutterstock Images, p. 6; © Everett Historical/Shutterstock Images, p. 7; Library of Congress,
p. 9; © Photo Researchers/Alamy Stock Photo, pp. 10, 16; © Everett Collection Historical/Alamy
Stock Photo, p. 11; © Lawrence Berkeley Nat'l Lab, pp. 12, 14; US Army Corps of Engineers, p. 19;
© Gjon Mili/The LIFE Picture Collection/Getty Images, p. 20; © Robert W. Kelley/The LIFE Picture
Collection/Getty Images, p. 22; © Smithsonian Institution Archives Image #SIA2010-1508, p. 23;
© Smithsonian Institution Archives Image #SIA2010-1507, p. 25; © Emilio Segrè Visual Archives/
American Institute of Physics/Science Source, p. 27.

Front Cover: © Smithsonian Institution Archives Image #SIA2010-1509.

CONTENTS

As a girl in the 1920s, Chien-Shiung had to work hard to get the same education as boys her age.

SCIENTIFIC START

Chien-Shiung Wu was born on May 29, 1912, in the small town of Liuhe, China. Chien-Shiung's parents encouraged her and her two brothers to read and ask questions about everything. In the evenings, her father, Zong-Yi, read news about the latest scientific discoveries to the whole family.

At that time, there were not many schools for girls in China. Most girls were taught only how to become good wives and mothers. But Chien-Shiung's father founded the Ming De School. This was the first girls' school in the region. Chien-Shiung's mother, Fuhua Fan, helped Zong-Yi convince other parents to send their daughters to the school.

When she was old enough, Chien-Shiung attended Ming De. But the school had only four grades. Chien-Shiung graduated when she was nine. She wanted to continue her education, but there were no other schools for girls in the area.

AWAY FROM HOME

Chien-Shiung applied to the Soochow Girls School in the city of Suzhou. This school was 50 miles (80 kilometers) from her home. For the next seven years, she saw her family only during school breaks.

The Soochow Girls School had two programs. One was a regular school, and the other was a teacher-training school. The teacher-training school was free. Students were promised a job after graduation. Chien-Shiung's family had enough money to pay for the regular school. But she wanted the challenge of the more difficult teacher-training program.

Chien-Shiung soon found that her friends in the regular school were learning more science than she was. She borrowed their textbooks. Sometimes she stayed up late at night. She taught herself math, physics, and chemistry. Soon,

Suzhou is located in eastern China, near Shanghai.

Marie Curie won two Nobel prizes for her groundbreaking work in physics and chemistry.

Chien-Shiung had a clear favorite subject: physics. At the time, physicists were making exciting discoveries about **atoms**. Chien-Shiung especially admired Marie Curie, a Polish-French physicist famous for discovering **radioactive elements**.

HEAD OF THE CLASS

In 1930, Chien-Shiung graduated from Soochow at the top of her class. She was chosen to attend the National Central

University in Nanjing. Chien-Shiung wanted to enroll in the school's physics program. But she was afraid she was too far behind in math and science. She spent the summer studying advanced math, chemistry, and physics. By the end of the summer, she was sure she could keep up.

Chien-Shiung did not just keep up. She excelled, becoming the top student in all her classes. As at Soochow, she spent late nights studying. She also spent time in the lab running experiments. In 1934, Chien-Shiung graduated with top honors. For the next year, she served as a teaching assistant at Zhejiang University in Hangzhou. Then she worked as a researcher at the National Academy of Sciences in Shanghai.

Still, Chien-Shiung wanted to learn more. But China offered no advanced programs in physics. So she packed her bags for the United States.

TECH TALK

"I have always felt that in physics, and probably in other endeavors, too, you must have total commitment. It is not just a job. It is a way of life."

–Chien-Shiung Wu

Shanghai was a bustling city with new industries in the early 1900s.

Chapter 2

Wu arrived in the United States ready to learn more about nuclear physics.

GOING
NUCLEAR

Wu traveled by ship to the United States. She arrived in California in August 1936. The twenty-four-year-old student planned to study at the University of Michigan. But she learned that women there were not allowed to use the

The cyclotron at Berkeley was the most powerful atom smasher in the world in the 1940s.

student union building without a male escort. She began looking at another college.

The University of California at Berkeley was more welcoming to women. In addition, it had one of the top **nuclear physics** programs in the country. Some of the best scientists of the time taught and researched there. Among them was Ernest Lawrence, inventor of the cyclotron. This machine accelerated atoms and smashed them together. J. Robert Oppenheimer was also at Berkeley. He would later be instrumental in the creation of the atomic bomb.

Emilio Segrè began working at the university's radiation laboratory in Livermore, California, in 1938.

Although the school term had already started, Wu applied to Berkeley's graduate program in physics. She was accepted. Soon, she began working with Emilio Segrè, one of Lawrence's assistants. Wu spent long hours doing research in the lab. She studied how particles passing through matter give off energy. Often, she did not go home until three o'clock in the morning.

FISSION PHYSICS

In 1938, scientists in Germany discovered nuclear fission. In this process, the **nucleus** of an atom splits. Splitting the nuclei of some atoms, such as uranium, releases huge amounts of energy.

Like other physicists, Wu was fascinated by fission. Working with Segrè, she began experiments on the products created during uranium fission. She discovered that one of the products was the gas xenon. This gas could produce the unwanted result of stopping the fission **chain reaction**. Wu's discovery would later be important in the development of the atomic bomb.

TECH TALK

"Chien-Shiung was very ambitious. She frequently quoted Madame Curie as her role model. She wanted to excel. I could feel her determination, and was confident that she could accomplish whatever she wanted."

–Robert Wilson, a Berkeley classmate

Segrè, Oppenheimer, and Wu (*from left to right*) attend dinner at the International House at Berkeley in 1939.

Wu received her PhD in physics from Berkeley in 1940. Afterward, she remained there as a research assistant. She continued to study fission reactions, and others considered her an expert in the field. Although Segrè wanted Berkeley to hire Wu, she was not offered a position on the faculty. Like the other top research schools of the time, Berkeley was unwilling to hire a woman to teach physics. Science was still considered a man's field.

TECH TALK

"You must know the purpose of the research exactly, what you want to get out of it, and what point you want to show."

–Chien-Shiung Wu

Chapter 3

Wu tests particles in the lab at Columbia.

WAR WORK

In 1942, Wu married Luke Yuan, a fellow Chinese physicist at Berkeley. The two moved to the East Coast. Wu took a position teaching physics at Smith College, a small women's school in Massachusetts. Although she enjoyed teaching, she

was not completely happy in her new role. She had little time or funding to conduct research, her first love.

Wu continued to attend physics conferences. At one, she met with her former Berkeley advisor, Ernest Lawrence. Afterward, Lawrence sent letters to several universities on her behalf. Soon, Wu had many job offers. Princeton University, Brown University, Harvard University, the Massachusetts Institute of Technology, and Columbia University all wanted her to work for them. Many of these schools did not accept female students or hire female instructors. But the country had recently entered World War II (1939–1945). Many of the nation's top physicists had been recruited to work on new technologies for the war effort. Physics professors were in high demand.

In 1943, Wu accepted a position at Princeton, becoming the school's first-ever female instructor. There, she taught physics to naval officers in the school's engineering program. She still had no opportunity to conduct her own research.

TOP SECRET

Soon after she started at Princeton, Columbia's Division of War Research contacted Wu. Physicists there interviewed her. They were careful not to tell her anything about the top-secret project they were working on. At the end of the interview, the physicists asked Wu if she could guess what their project was. She said yes. From the formulas written on the blackboards, she knew they were working on an atomic bomb. She was asked to start the next day.

Wu began working at Columbia in March 1944. Wu was chosen to join the Manhattan Project. This was the United States' secret program dedicated to creating an atomic bomb. Wu's role involved producing uranium to undergo a fission reaction in the bomb. Wu also developed sensitive radiation detectors. Her old Berkeley paper on the effects of xenon helped other members of the Manhattan Project with problems in chain reactions. On July 16, 1945, the first successful atomic bomb was tested.

AN EXPERT IN THE FIELD

After the war ended in 1945, Wu was one of the few physicists asked to remain as a researcher at Columbia. She decided to study beta decay. This is a form of radioactivity. It occurs when **electrons** are ejected from the nucleus of an atom. In 1933, Enrico Fermi had theorized that some electrons would burst out of the nucleus at high speeds during beta decay. But so

Oppenheimer (*left*) and Manhattan Project director Leslie Groves (*right*) examine the Trinity test site in New Mexico after the first successful atomic bomb test.

Wu was a dedicated researcher and demanding teacher at Columbia in the 1950s.

far, experiments had not confirmed this. Many scientists had recorded only slow-moving electrons in beta decay.

Wu read everything she could find about the earlier experiments. She found that most had tested radioactive materials that were thick and uneven. This slowed down the electrons as they were ejected. Wu designed her own experiment using thin, uniform samples of radioactive materials. Her results proved Fermi's theory. By the early 1950s, she was considered the foremost expert in beta decay.

In 1952, Wu was made an associate professor at Columbia. She used much of her own research in teaching her courses. She expected the same precision and dedication from her students as she did from herself.

TECH TALK

"Students will not become great scientists by taking lectures, memorizing formulae, or doing routine experiments. It is more important to develop a habit of investigation, risk-taking, and the ability to observe and deduce."

–Chien-Shiung Wu, 1967 speech

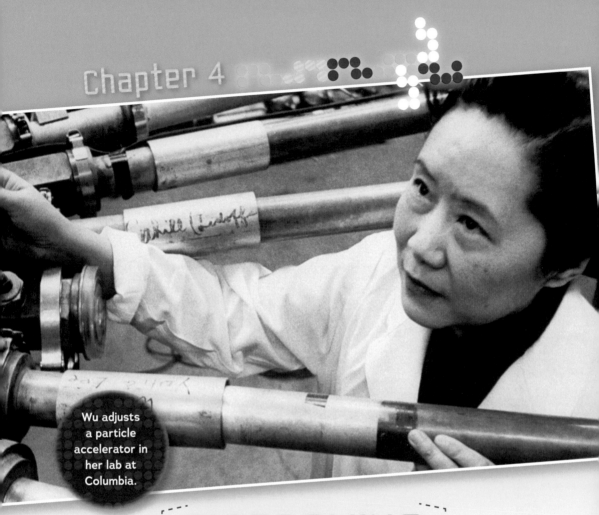

Chapter 4

Wu adjusts a particle accelerator in her lab at Columbia.

DISPROVING A LAW

Throughout the 1950s, physicists continued to smash atoms. They studied the resulting parts, known as subatomic particles. Physicists believed that everything that happened in the nucleus of an atom was symmetrical, or equal on both sides. This concept was known as the law of conservation of parity. Parity meant that if you looked at a mirror image of a particle, it would behave the same as the particle did in real life. The only difference would be that left and right were reversed. For example, think of looking in a mirror while spinning with your arm over your head. If you spin to the right, your mirror image will appear to spin to the left. But your arm will still be over your head. If a particle undergoing radioactive decay spins to the left, its mirror image spins to the right. But each should still give off the same number of electrons upward and downward.

In 1956, researchers Tsung-Dao Lee of Columbia and Chen Ning Yang of the Institute for Advanced Study came to

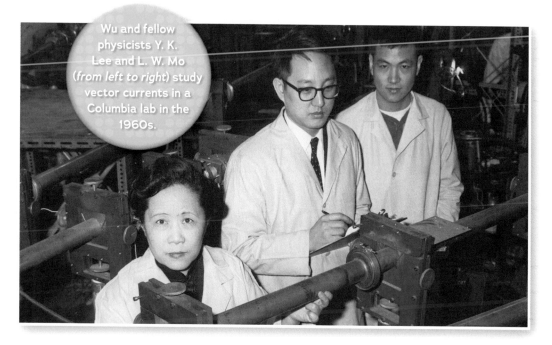

Wu and fellow physicists Y. K. Lee and L. W. Mo (*from left to right*) study vector currents in a Columbia lab in the 1960s.

Wu. They had been studying a newly discovered subatomic particle that did not seem to behave symmetrically. After reading hundreds of pages of research, the scientists found that the law of conservation of parity had never been proved through experiments.

Wu did not think the law was likely to be disproved. But without experimental results, they might never know if the law held up. So Wu spent months designing an experiment to test it. She created much of the equipment for the experiment herself.

THE RESULTS ARE IN

Wu's experiment examined the beta decay of radioactive cobalt. As with all elements, cobalt's atoms are constantly moving. Wu needed to slow them down so she could observe them. To do this, she had to cool the cobalt to near

TECH TALK

"This small modest woman was powerful enough to do what armies can never accomplish: she helped destroy a law of nature."

–New York Post, *January 22, 1959*

Wu conducts an experiment with a particle accelerator at Columbia University in 1963.

"It is the courage to doubt what has long been established, the incessant search for its verification and proof, that pushed the wheel of science forward."

—Chien-Shiung Wu, 1957

absolute zero, approximately –460°F (–273.15 °C). This is the temperature at which all motion stops. The National Bureau of Standards in Washington, DC, was one of the few labs in the country that could cool substances to near absolute zero. Wu conducted her experiments there. Once the cobalt was cooled, it was placed in a powerful magnetic field. This made the cobalt atoms' nuclei line up. Wu could then observe the direction traveled by the ejected electrons.

Wu repeated her experiment several times. In the end, the results were certain. When the direction of the nucleus's spin changed, the electrons were emitted in different directions. They were not mirror images. The law of conservation of parity did not always hold.

Columbia University hosted a press conference on January 15, 1957, to announce the results. Major newspapers and magazines, including the *New York Times*, *Time*, and *Life*, covered the discovery. The world was stunned to learn that a major law of physics had been disproved.

LASTING LEGACY

Lee and Yang were awarded the 1957 Nobel Prize in Physics for the discovery. Because she had not come up with the

Wu earned the American Physical Society award in nuclear physics in 1975.

theory, Wu did not share in the prize. Although she was disappointed, she continued her research. Wu later proved two other laws of nuclear physics.

Although she never won a Nobel Prize, Wu received many other awards. In 1975, she became the first female president of the American Physical Society. Three years later, she was awarded the first-ever Wolf Prize. Wu also received the National Medal of Science, the highest science award in the United States.

Throughout her life, Wu encouraged women to pursue careers in the sciences. Her work in physics led to important breakthroughs. After her death on February 16, 1997, she left behind a legacy showing how much women could achieve in nuclear physics.

TIMELINE

1912

Chien-Shiung Wu is born in Liuhe, China on May 29.

1934

Wu graduates from China's National Central University.

1936

Wu travels to the United States and begins her studies at the University of California, Berkeley.

1938

German and Austrian scientists discover nuclear fission, and Wu begins to study fission products.

1940

Wu receives her PhD in physics from Berkeley.

1943

Wu becomes the first female instructor at Princeton University.

1944

Wu joins the Division of War Research at Columbia University in March, working on the development of the atomic bomb.

1957

Wu announces the results of her experiment disproving the law of conservation of parity on January 15.

1975

Wu becomes the first female president of the American Physical Society.

1997

Wu dies at the age of eighty-four on February 16.

SOURCE NOTES

8 Sharon Bertsch McGrayne, *Nobel Prize Women in Science: Their Lives, Struggles, and Momentous Discoveries* (Washington, DC: Joseph Henry, 1998), 263–64.

13 McGrayne, *Nobel Prize Women in Science*, 268.

15 Chiang Tsai-Chien, *Madame Wu Chien-Shiung: The First Lady of Physics Research* (Hackensack, NJ: World Scientific, 2014), 90.

21 Tsai-Chien, *Madame Wu Chien-Shiung*, 251.

24 Rachel Swaby, *Headstrong: 52 Women Who Changed Science—and the World* (New York: Broadway Books, 2015), 146.

26 Lisa Yount, *A to Z of Women in Science and Math* (New York: Facts on File, 1999), 216.

GLOSSARY

atoms
the smallest units of an element

chain reaction
a reaction that creates energy, which causes another of the same kind of reaction

electrons
small particles surrounding the nucleus that have a negative electrical charge

elements
substances made up of only one kind of atom

nuclear physics
the branch of science that studies the nucleus of atoms

nucleus
the central part of an atom

radioactive
giving off energy as atoms break apart

FURTHER

INFORMATION

BOOKS

Hammond, Richard. *Chien-Shiung Wu: Pioneering Nuclear Physicist.* New York: Chelsea House, 2010. Read more about Chien-Shiung Wu's work as a nuclear physicist.

Krull, Kathleen. *Lives of the Scientists: Experiments, Explosions (and What the Neighbors Thought).* Boston: Harcourt, 2013. Discover other famous scientists who made an impact on the scientific world.

Wheeler, Jill C. *Chien-Shiung Wu: Phenomenal Physicist.* Minneapolis, MN: Abdo, 2013. This biography covers Chien-Shiung Wu's family, childhood, and work.

WEBSITES

Famous Female Scientists: Chien-Shiung Wu
http://famousfemalescientists.com/chien-shiung-wu
Learn more about Chien-Shiung Wu, including her early life and her honors.

National Women's Hall of Fame
https://www.womenofthehall.org/inductee/chienshiung-wu
Read a short biography of Wu and her work.

Physics4Kids: Nuclear Physics
http://www.physics4kids.com/files/mod_nuc.html
Discover more about nuclear physics, the subject Wu spent her life researching.

INDEX

ABOUT THE AUTHOR

Valerie Bodden has written more than 200 nonfiction books for children. Her books have received positive reviews from *School Library Journal*, *Booklist*, *Children's Literature*, *ForeWord Magazine*, *Horn Book Guide*, *VOYA*, and *Library Media Connection*. Bodden lives in Wisconsin with her husband and four young children.